About The [Author]

Terry Quinn began his career [as a Financial Consultant] within a High Street Bank and was a consistent prize winner, quickly becoming the top producer in Scotland. His reputation was so well-respected within the Bank that he was a regular speaker at seminars and conferences. He was proud to be unanimously chosen by the Regional Directors of the bank to address his fellow colleagues on Integrity in 'Working Practise' where there were over three thousand in attendance.

His career progressed as an Independent Financial Adviser for many years before being recruited by a major insurance company and was again the top sole trader within his first year.

Terry has been in Financial Services for over fifteen years and provides a wealth of experience, which has involved arranging thousands of mortgages, savings plans and investments amounting to over £40 million pounds.

Terry currently has a successful financial practice and estate agency in the town of Largs, Ayrshire in Scotland.

He is a powerful and gifted communicator and is passionate about "Life Application Teaching to the Body of Christ".

Throughout the UK, Terry has shared his own powerful testimony of God's restoring power and is a graduate of Rhema bible college. He believes there are "season in God" (Ecclesiastes 3:1-2) and he believes there was indeed a time and season for teaching the principles of biblical prosperity. Today, however, is the season to take the next step. NOW is the time for the body of Christ to be equipped with the principles of practical prosperity.

Practical Prosperity Publications

© Terry Quinn, 2005

The moral right of the author has been asserted.
All rights reserved. No part of this publication may be reproduced or transmitted in any form or by any means, electronic or mechanical, including photocopying, recording or any information storage or retrieval system, without prior permission in writing from the publishers.

First published in 2005

Practical Prosperity Publications
Largs
Ayrshire
Scotland
KA30 8EJ

Tel: 01475 686 202
http://www.practicalprosperity.co.uk

British Library Cataloguing in Publication Data.
A catalogue record of this book
is available from the British Library.

ISBN 0 9551427 0 9

Printed and bound in Great Britain

Acknowledgements

I would like to thank my darling wife Alison
for painstakingly proof reading all the material
contained in this book. Your encouragement, patience,
and sensitivity during the writing was so appreciated,
and the end product is a tribute to your literacy skills.

To my son Danny, who created the book cover –
thank you son for your desire to please me –
I know I can be a challenge but your attitude and
understanding always amazes me.

To my dear friends John and Tricia Edwards –
thank you for all your encouragement and support.
We have been through good and bad times together
and your agape love is engraved in my heart.

To my brother Paul – thanks for your love
and laughter when I most needed it.

To Alec and Lilia Muir, of whom I am so
proud to be associated with; Alec you have
always stood by me and have been a true friend.

To my pastor Paul Scanlon –
your teaching and wisdom has been
a source of strength and much needed
encouragement at the lowest point of my life.

Most of all, I thank my Jesus
for never leaving me, nor forsaking me.

Dedication

I dedicate this book to my parents
who have been such a great example
of selfless love throughout my life.

To my mum I say:

"YOUR GOLDEN BOY IS NOW AN AUTHOR"

To my dad I say:

"YOUR BROKEN BOY IS WHOLE AGAIN"

Foreword

I have known Terry Quinn for years and have witnessed his life going from mountain top to valley and back again. He's shown himself to be a man who understands brokenness and humility, and yet has the boldness to arise and be heard.

In this book that Terry has written I have been truly blessed by how he was able to concisely and creatively bring an amazing and simple clarity to the whole topic of Biblical prosperity and God's will towards finance and His people. Scripture tells us that a false balance is an abomination to the Lord, but a just weight is His delight. Correct weights and values are of ultimate importance to the Lord, and Terry has defined and wonderfully honed some "weights" that we can all accurately measure by in regards to this topic.

In keeping his writing short, he's made it simple for us all to digest, and I'm sure that you who read it will feel the witness of God's Spirit upon it. You'll also find yourself quoting many of the statements Terry writes.

After reading this I pray that Terry will set his hand to the task again and give us more to digest in years to come. I highly recommend this book.

Rod Anderson

Founder/Director
Prayer for the Nations

Introduction

I would like to state right at the very beginning of this book, that it is my heart filled desire to bring the *balance to biblical prosperity principles* and to fill the gap which I feel is so necessary for the Church of Jesus Christ.

This book has been birthed through my own personal experiences of attending prosperity conferences and in a professional capacity, having to counsel hundreds of Christians on financial matters.

Having been brought up to believe that poverty was 'Godly' and that the 'rich' were in some way not fully accepted in the body of Christ, I was liberated to hear of biblical prosperity being taught to the church. I attended many seminars, studied the material and listened to all of the tapes. I was blessed and encouraged that at last I was being taught that God was not against money or possessions. I subsequently embraced this neglected revelation with passion and became a serious giver into many ministries with great joy in my heart.

However, I now feel strongly, that I must address many issues which are heavy on my heart for God's people, and the subsequent pain many have felt and experienced. I have personally witnessed many Christians returning

BALANCING PROSPERITY PRINCIPLES

from some prosperity seminars so excited and enthusiastic but with *no practical knowledge* on *how* to prosper. I have met and spoken to hundreds of Gods people who are so genuine in their devotion and want to demonstrate their love of God by becoming generous givers. However, there are so many who are still no further forward financially, despite attending such seminars, and have never experienced the *breakthrough* promised by the biblical message. I believe that this topic is the source of so much controversy within the body of Christ, because so far we have only heard the *spiritual principle message* with little or no practical outworking or follow up. The people of God are left feeling terrible *guilt and inadequacy*, because the messages they heard, promised increase and abundance within their finances. This in turn, may lead to *confusion and discouragement*.

God must have an answer to this!!

I believe we must have balance in our approach to prosperity which involves God's wisdom and not just a formula to 'get rich quick'. I do however wish to emphasise strongly that my aim is to redress this balance and not to cause anymore confusion. I am aware that many are even offended by biblical prosperity teaching and have become bitter and angry. If you are one of these people, let me first of all say that what you are feeling is ok. It is perfectly natural to be hurt by the manipulative tactics displayed by *some* preachers and indeed, your pain is part of the process of healing. However I would caution you not to stay in that place of pain, as you will never experience real joy and contentment when harbouring these feelings.

Pastors and preachers are not perfect and I believe that the majority are not purposely trying to hurt or confuse through any teaching or principle. Pray for them, love them, bless them and most of all keep your eyes on **Jesus**.

Contents

FOREWORD — Page vii

INTRODUCTION — Page ix

CHAPTER ONE — Page 1
Materialism, Money and Success

CHAPTER TWO — Page 5
Manna, Prosperity and Harvest Prosperity

CHAPTER THREE — Page 9
Prosperity is a Process

CHAPTER FOUR — Page 11
The Application of Wisdom

CHAPTER FIVE — Page 17
Balancing the Prosperity Scriptures

CHAPTER SIX — Page 23
Parallel Truth –
Learn how the Enemy divides the Scriptures

CHAPTER SEVEN — Page 29
Faith or Foolishness

CHAPTER EIGHT   Page 39
Don't Give the Devil a Foothold

CHAPTER NINE   Page 43
Why are Christians not Prospering?

CHAPTER TEN   Page 47
Prosper by Grace not by Law

CHAPTER ELEVEN   Page 55
Seek Wise Counsel and Knowledge
Not a Formula

CHAPTER TWELVE   Page 67
A Dose of Reality

CONCLUSION   Page 73
Balancing the Prosperity Scriptures

INDEX   Page 75
Scriptures on Biblical Principles
and Practical Prosperity

Chapter 1
Materialism, Money and Success

One of the most difficult areas for most Christians to deal with is this whole area of *'having things'*. I have witnessed so many being hurt, feeling confused and guilty by their own understanding of God's view on prosperity. Well-intended speakers setting out biblical principles have omitted from their message, the practical application of prosperity with the focus being 'purely spiritual' and the emphasis being that our prosperity is only for the furtherance of the Gospel.

God's View

Many people have asked me over the years "What's God's view on the subject of money?" Does God want us to have it?

The Simple answer is **Yes**

Blessings for Practical Reasons

The main focus of Biblical Prosperity teaching has been that God wants to bless us so we can sow into ministries and the spreading of the Gospel, which is true – in part. However, God being a Father **wants to bless us** unselfishly <u>first</u> and <u>foremost</u>.

BALANCING PROSPERITY PRINCIPLES

We are required in life to participate in material things apart from Church:

- **We need clothes**
- **We need to pay our bills**
- **We need to feed our family**
- **We need good jobs**
- **We need holidays**
- **We need to save for the future**
- **We need to protect our family**
- **We need good functional cars**

'Don't be forced into spiritualising everything to do with your prosperity'

God's Practical View from the Beginning

In the Garden of Eden, God looked around and showed Adam and Eve everything He had given them. Notice they had not given to God first to allow Him to bless them. God as Creator and Father gives to His children out of love. God showed Adam and Eve everything that he had given them

> *The Lord God took the man and put him in the Garden of Eden to work it and take care of it.*
> **Genesis 2:15**

I want to show you from this scripture the balance between Spiritual Provision and Practical Prosperity Teaching.

In the first instance God blessed Adam and Eve with an abundance of Provision, however He required of them to:

- **Work it**
- **Take care of it**
- **Tend it**
- **Cultivate the soil**

Although it does not directly make mention of it in this scripture, I believe that God must have provided the tools and utensils to hoe the ground and till the soil.

Practical Prosperity Tools

Notice here the balance between Spiritual and Practical Prosperity in the Garden of Eden. God had provided but had required Adam to *apply practical skills* in order to bring the land under subjection. God put him there, gave him a business and employment and then required Adam *to do his bit, by physically working*.

Before The Fall

It is easy to miss out the fact that God had required this of Adam from the beginning, as we tend to focus on the curse that came after the fall mentioned in Genesis 3:17:-

> To Adam He said – *Because you listened to your wife and ate from tree about which I commanded you, you must not eat of it. Cursed is the ground because of you. Through painful toil, you will eat of it all the days of your life.*

However God actually asked Adam and Eve to work *prior* to the fall.

This paradise was not an exemption from work but God in his provision had left room for improvement by *practical* application.

The Balance

We can conclude from Genesis that Biblical and Practical Prosperity Principles were aligned from the beginning of creation.

Chapter 2
Manna Prosperity and Harvest Prosperity

I want to point out in this chapter, another time in biblical history in which we see God's provision, and what He requires of his people. This is to demonstrate the balance of Prosperity Principles.

In the first instance, I would liken Biblical Prosperity Principles to the Manna, which was provided by God to the people of Israel in the wilderness. At this point, let me provide the background information required in order to gain understanding.

The people of Israel had been led out of slavery and of poverty, which I believe happened when God anointed Biblical Prosperity Teaching

The Church received *neglected revelation* of God's view of prosperity and money. Satan had kept us bound in darkness and in debt and then God provided this 'Spiritual Manna', which was to feed God's People. However, coming out of poverty and slavery is only a *part of God's plan for us*.

Manna Miracles taught Gods people to *seek him first*, to trust in his provision and to gather their food on a daily basis, teaching them that God truly cares and supplies their daily bread.

BALANCING PROSPERITY PRINCIPLES

When the people of Israel left Egypt and crossed the Red Sea, this was an *exit*, an escape from slavery, however when they crossed the Jordan, it was *entrance*. An invasion into new territory. In the past they were delivered from dominion and oppression, now they were to have dominion *over* their enemies

The liberating message of biblical prosperity demonstrated the same principle of 'coming out'. However, I believe Practical Prosperity Principles demonstrates 'going in'. The Red Sea was symbolic of *'stepping out'* but the Jordan was *'stepping in'*

Faith and Works

God wants us to believe daily for our needs – God wants us to trust Him, but Manna Miracles were the easiest from a human participation point of view. Manna didn't involve a battle to possess or require hard work to cultivate the soil; no ploughing, weeding, watering or harvesting.

Manna Miracles Only Require:

- **To wake up**
- **To pick up**
- **It only provides enough to feed the one who partakes**

However, Harvest Miracles:

Require practical application of God's trust and hard work. They nourish not only the one who partakes but multiplied, others as well. I believe that the Church is at a crossroads today in the area of prosperity. The realisation has come that harvesting and farming require *hard work and practical application*. However, this also requires as much of a miracle as receiving manna.

MANNA PROSPERITY AND HARVEST PROSPERITY

Move On

We need this balance and I place a challenge before those who read this book. *It is time to move on! Stop expecting and relying on Manna Miracles. Instead learn to cultivate, weed, water and harvest.* It is time for the Church to move. God wants us to learn a way of life that is not dependant on 'Manna Miracles' to sustain our faith. He wants us to learn and *possess his promises* for prosperity and this requires *growth and maturity.*

Chapter 3
Prosperity is a Process

There are three stages of prosperity, which I mentioned earlier, that are paralleled in the Exodus of the People of Israel.

- Egypt (not enough)
- The Wilderness (just enough)
- Canaan (more than enough)

Egypt

God's chosen people crossed the Red Sea laden with gold, silver, jewels and the finest garments which were all given to them by the Egyptians.

This teaches us that as you *break out* of the slavery of poverty thinking, God will reward us with financial blessings, which is the start of the *process*.

Wilderness

God provided water from the rock, bread from the sky and fresh quail. He taught them to live day-by-day trusting in His provision but this was not their inheritance, however it was still part of the *process*

BALANCING PROSPERITY PRINCIPLES

You may be in the wilderness at the moment, living from day to day, week to week but remember this is an important part of the *process* and a necessary part of learning in the area of prosperity.

Many have made the mistake of trying to *jump from Egypt to Canaan* after attending a prosperity seminar with disastrous consequences.

The wilderness is important because you learn to walk consistently with God and in the principles of faith. So that when God does bless you with abundance, you have learnt to look to *Him* as your source and not to a formula or set of rules.

Canaan

> *When the Lord your God brings you into the land he swore to your Fathers, to Abraham, Isaac and Jacob, to give you a land with large flourishing cities you did not build, houses filled with all kinds of good things you did not provide, wells you did not dig and vineyards and olive groves you did not plant. Then, when you eat and are satisfied, be careful that you do not forget the Lord who brought you out of Egypt, out of the land of slavery*
>
> ***Deut 6-10-12***

However the wilderness is not the place God wants you to stay. God desires you to come into Canaan where you will be greatly blessed. This represents God's promise to his people who have the *full balance* of God's prosperity principles in place. This is the kind of prosperity God has in his heart for his people. It only comes because you go after God *and* his **Wisdom**.

Chapter 4

The Application of Wisdom

Although Solomon is recorded as having vast wealth and prosperity he is remembered most for his **WISDOM**.

His building programme and his wealth generated through trade and administrative reorganisation culminated in his most famous project, God's Temple. In the story of Solomon we see a balanced picture of prosperity. In the first instance Solomon sought God with humility not asking for wealth and riches but wisdom.

> *At Gibeon, the Lord appeared to Solomon during the night in a dream and God said, **"Ask for whatever you want me to give you".***
> *Solomon answered "You have shown great kindness to your servant, my Father, David because he was faithful to you and righteous and upright in heart. You have continued this great kindness to him and have given him a son to sit on his throne this very day. Now oh Lord my God, you have made your servant King, in place of my Father David. But I am only a little child and do not know how to carry out my duties. Your servant is here among the people you have chosen, a great people, too numerous to count or number. **So give your servant a discerning***

BALANCING PROSPERITY PRINCIPLES

> *heart to govern your people and to distinguish between right and wrong. For who is able to govern this great people of yours".*
>
> *The Lord was pleased that Solomon had asked for this, so God said to him "Since you have asked for this and not for long life or wealth for yourself, nor have asked for the death of your enemies but for wisdom in administering justice, I will do what you have asked. **I will give you a wise and discerning heart**, so that there will never have been anyone like you, nor will there ever be. Moreover I will give you what you have not asked for. Both riches and honour so that in your life time, you will have no equal among Kings and if you walk in my ways, and obey my statutes and commands as David your Father did, I will give you a long life"*
>
> **1st KINGS 3:v5-14**

The servants heart that Solomon displayed, pleased God who throughout scripture gives servanthood the highest priority.

> *Jesus called them together and said "You know that the rulers of the gentiles Lord it over them and their high officials exercise authority over them. Not so with you. **Instead, whoever wants to become great among you must be your servant** and whoever wants to be first, must be your slave. Just as the Son of Man did not come to be served but to serve and to give His life as a ransom for many"*
>
> **Math 20:v25-28**

> *When He had finished washing their feet, he put on his clothes and returned to His place. "Do you understand what I have done for you" He asked them. "You call me Teacher and Lord and rightly*

THE APPLICATION OF WISDOM

so for that is what I am. Now that I your Lord and Teacher have washed your feet, you also should wash one another's feet. I have set you an example, that you should do as I have done for you. I tell you the truth, no servant is greater than his master, nor is a messenger greater than the one who sent him. Now that you know these things, you will be blessed if you do them"
John 13:v12-17

Solomon demonstrated practical application *and* God's wisdom working together. Let us not make the error of supposing a person who knows a lot is therefore wise. The wise person applies what he knows to make right and good decisions and *serving* is true evidence of God's authority in our lives. The missing part in balancing prosperity principles is the application of **wisdom**. I have witnessed so many people who desire prosperity but have no *'common sense'*. They rush into applying biblical principles, expecting God to open the windows of Heaven and change their financial situation overnight. Too many have treated this type of application as an instant *'get rich quick scheme'*. However prosperity is a *way of life*; it is acting on what you believe. Let me explain by way of an illustration:

We all know that we need food for our bodies, but you could *starve to death* in the middle of a supermarket if you don't eat. However, there is a practical process which has to be put in place that will keep you from starving. The process is, that you have to *go* to the check out, *pay* for the food and *then* eat it.

We cannot expect to prosper when we don't seek God's wisdom in practical ways. The heavy emphasis of God seeking to bless us is only *half of the picture*. I am very concerned by the *lack of balance* in teaching God's people. They have been given great hope by prosperity teaching

BALANCING PROSPERITY PRINCIPLES

but when *too much* is expected *too soon,* hope can wane and *faith evaporates*. We need to trust GOD and learn his ways for our own practical financial situation, which in some cases can take years, so we need to keep our eyes on the *promise not the calendar*.

Natural and Spiritual

This process can be demonstrated in nature and can be reflected in the same way in our own spiritual lives.

Consider:

- **The growth of a plant**
- **The forming of a flower**
- **The perfecting of a fruit**

Compared to:

- **The growth of a soul**
- **The transformation of a life**
- **The fruit of a life changed**

Mystery and Miracle

How does a rose become a rose?

The fact remains that science is baffled by this phenomenon – we only know *what we have to apply* to the seed in order for it to *be transformed* into a beautiful flower. It needs to *be planted* in the right kind of soil, exposed to the sun, watered regularly and kept in an open space to receive plenty of air.

The result of this *practical application* is a rich looking plant with beautiful petals and a lovely fragrance. It is the same with the field clothed with corn and trees laden with fruit, the colours, the fragrance, the taste, this is no accident but

THE APPLICATION OF WISDOM

a direct result of man's co-operation with nature. Spiritual parallels are the same. When we are exposed to the Word, Worship, Fellowship and study we are transformed. There is no short cut to natural fruit and spiritual fruit. A man or woman, experiencing great fruit in their lives will be *disciplined* in Prayer, Fellowship, study and Worship.

The next time you pass a beautiful garden or a farm with a harvest you will know that somebody has been *working, toiling and sweating it out behind the scenes*.

I have to conclude this chapter with an impassioned plea not to expect a **'quick'** breakthrough in your finances. Contrary to some teaching, the fact remains that stamping on your bills, will *not* make them go away!

DO NOT REJECT THE TRUTH

At this point I feel it is prudent to note a word of warning as I know many, many Christians have been hurt and disillusioned with prosperity teaching and in particular prosperity teachers. I regret to admit it but I can see why there may be those who may have an issue, in particular, with *some* preachers for the way they have presented prosperity to the Body of Christ. It appears that the majority who preach this message project an image of wealth and indeed it may seem that they are the only ones who are living in abundance.

In the UK in particular, I have been saddened that even the media have **mocked** the TV evangelists considering them to be tricking the people of God to make **themselves wealthy.** However it is a big mistake to reject the truth of God's message regardless of the vessel.

I believe that we do need a *healthy approach*, and to bury our head in the sand without highlighting the problems the Body of Christ has encountered, would be remiss of

BALANCING PROSPERITY PRINCIPLES

all of us and, therefore, I have decided to make these points to identify how many Christians *feel* and not to point the finger at any Minister of the Gospel.

Chapter 5

Balancing the Prosperity Scriptures

I have been so concerned in the area of misunderstood texts within prosperity teaching. Therefore I aim to cover these in detail to bring **balance** and **insight** which I hope will help many people.

Owe No Man Anything

> *Let no debt remain outstanding, except the continuing debt to love one another. For he who loves his fellow man has fulfilled the law.*
> ***Romans 13v8***

This scripture has been quoted to me so many times by well-meaning Christians who really desire to obey God's will but find themselves *confused* by its meaning. They think that it means they can't take out mortgages, personal loans or even credit cards.

In the first instance, I would like to point out that there is great danger in taking a scripture *out of context*. Doing so places many of God's people in bondage. The history of the church is full of well-intentioned Christians taking the *wrong meaning* from a scripture. This process has impacted on the lives of thousands in denominations all over the world.

BALANCING PROSPERITY PRINCIPLES

Subjects such as:

- **Music**
- **Baptism**
- **Communion**
- **Healing**
- **Spiritual Gifts**
- **Head Covering**
- **Women's Ministry**

I would like to fuse two scriptures together to bring balance and insight into the discovering of God's word.

> *Now the Lord is the Spirit and where the Spirit of the Lord is, there is Liberty.*
> 2nd *Cor 3v17*

> *Let peace be your umpire.*
> *Col 3v15*

I have found in my personal walk with God that these two scriptures when fused together can bring *insight* and *clarity* into a situation which may leave me wondering which path to take.

The scripture tells us that the spirit of God will *lead us* into all truth (*John 16v13*) therefore we need his guidance when interpreting the scripture. A sure sign of his presence is *there is a feeling of Liberty and Peace.* In my experience I have counselled Christians who have had no peace and were in confusion as they try to obey the scriptures. Here is also, another scripture which I feel it prudent to add at this point:

> *God is not the author of confusion*
> *1st Cor 14v33*

Let's look at Romans 13 in context, not just one verse, this is where *error* may occur if the scriptures are not studied

BALANCING THE PROSPERITY SCRIPTURES

in a contextual fashion. The apostle Paul is writing to believers in the first instance making a number of important points he feels the need to get across.

In my bible the heading starts:
Submission to the Authorities

> *Every one must submit himself to governing authorities, for there is no authority except that which God has established. The authorities which exist have been established by God. Consequently he who rebels against authority is rebelling against what God has instituted and those who do so will bring judgement upon themselves.*
> **Romans 13v1-4**

Paul uses key words in the first few verses of this chapter exhorting the Romans to submit to authority and warns that those who rebel against the authority that God has established rebels against God. Now Paul is not writing about submitting to your pastor, minister or elder – but to **GOVERNMENT**.

Verse 6 and 7 Reads:

> *This is also why you pay taxes for the authorities are God's servants who give their full time to governing give everyone what you owe him. If you owe taxes, pay taxes, if revenue, then revenue, if respect then respect, if honour then honour.*

Therefore, when we now look at Verse 8 again, we can understand that *To* owe *no man anything*, has nothing to do with debt but simply to pay your tax bill

These scriptures speak about the believer's relationship with the governing authorities and to show them respect and honour. It is not a command *not to borrow*

BALANCING PROSPERITY PRINCIPLES

> *The borrower is servant to the lender*
> **Proverbs 22v7**

This is another scripture which has also been misused when dealing with borrowing for our necessities in life. I believe with all my heart that this should be our ultimate goal and we should never need to borrow but this can *take a long time*. However, it is totally unrealistic and unbiblical to impose this scripture on God's people, with the possibility of bringing them into bondage.

In the Old Testament God understood people would have to borrow and he addressed it extensively. God gave special laws about borrowing every seven years and also every fifty years (known as the Jubilee). The people of Israel were to cancel all debts.

> *At the end of every seven years you must cancel debts. This is how it is to be done. Every creditor shall cancel the loan he has made to his fellow Israelite. He shall not require payment from his fellow Israelite or brother, because "The Lord's time for cancelling debt has been proclaimed"*
> **Deuteronomy 15v1**

Let's look at other scriptures which proves that borrowing happened.

> *Evil men borrow and cannot pay it back but the good man returns what he owes with some extra besides.*
> **Psalm 37v21 (TLB)**

> *If a man borrows an animal from his neighbour and it is injured or dies while the owner is not present, he must make restitution.*
> **Exodus 22v14**

BALANCING THE PROSPERITY SCRIPTURES

As one of them was cutting down a tree, the iron axe-head fell into the water. "Oh My Lord" he cried out "It was borrowed.

2nd Kings 6v5

Chapter 6
Parallel Truth

The scripture also teaches that we must not be ignorant of the devils schemes, as he is a master at bringing confusion on God's people, in particular, when there is a <u>parallel truth.</u> Let me explain what I mean by this.

Many people will read (*Rom 13v8*) and take it at face value and interpret

> ***Owe no man anything means . . .***
> ***don't buy anything on credit***

Then comes the confusion and guilt and many believe that if they buy something on credit making monthly instalments they are in *violation* of God's word.

Truth in the bible that is presented in parallel, presents the devil with an opportunity to <u>distort</u>.

The enemy's no 1 target is God's word – we learn in Genesis:

- *He doubts*
- *He distorts*
- *He denies*

BALANCING PROSPERITY PRINCIPLES

He even tried this tactic on Jesus.

> *The devil led Him to Jerusalem and had Him stand on the highest point of the Temple. "If you are the son of God" he said. "Throw yourself down from here, for it is written 'He will command His angels concerning you, to guard you carefully. They will lift you up in their hands so that you will not strike your foot against a stone'" Jesus answered, "It is also written, do not put the Lord your God to the test"*
>
> **Luke 4:9-12**

Notice he *distorts* the scripture when quoting Psalm 91.

This scripture speaks about angelic protection however the devil tries to use this in order to trick Jesus into *wilful suicide* using the *half-truth* of the scriptures .His tactics have never changed. He failed with Jesus but has succeeded with the church.

Another scripture we see this same parallel is in **John 1v14**:

> *The Word became flesh and made His dwelling among us. We have seen His Glory, the Glory of the one and only who came from the Father full of **Grace** and **Truth**. We learn that Jesus is full of **Grace** and Truth.*

Notice the first glimpse we have of Jesus is *Grace* but we in the church have accentuated *The Truth*. The devil **has divided** this scripture very cleverly and Christians have majored on presenting Jesus:

- **As bringing the Truth of Judgement**
- **The Truth of Doctrine**
- **The Truth of Hell**

PARALLEL TRUTH

- **Jesus is seen as angry with the world.**

- **He is seen not as a friend of sinners.**

- **But a friend of the church and all who are holy and righteous.**

- **The lost are condemned to hell.**

- **The gospel becomes judgement**

That is why we don't see people rushing into church today because *The Half-Truth* of the gospel is being preached. Can you see how the enemy has used the scriptures to <u>divide</u> the full revelation of God? The *Truth* preached without being *Preceded by Grace is the Law – and the Law Failed.*

The apostle Paul warned the Galatian:

"You foolish Galatians, who has bewitched you"
(Gal 3v1)

This was in reference to Judaisers who were preaching observance to the law instead of Faith.

Circumcision was being presented as a truth but this was not *the whole truth*

The devil has *bewitched* the church in the area of prosperity.

So many today have been *side-tracked* by the enemy into believing a *half-truth*

Now returning to our opening scripture in (*Rom 13v8*) you will be able to read and understand the context and I will also point out other scriptures to bring the balance and full truth. If this scripture really meant we were not

BALANCING PROSPERITY PRINCIPLES

to borrow or buy anything in credit then why are there other scripture passages in the bible where *God requires you to loan money* or goods to somebody else. If it is wrong for me to borrow then it would be wrong for me to lend to someone else, because I would require them to borrow and pay back. That is why it is important to use other scriptures in order to clarify another. (*Matthew 5:42*)

This is Jesus speaking here:

> *"Give to the one who asks you and do not turn away from the one who wants to borrow from you". From this scripture we learn that if it is wrong for you to owe then why would Jesus tell you it is okay to lend to someone else thus causing them to owe you.*

If owing is wrong then it is wrong for everybody. If it is wrong for me to owe money or buy something on credit then it is *wrong* for me to put another man in *bondage by owing me*.

In my business I have dealt with hundreds of young married couples who are starting out in life and they need many things to build their new home. Although some receive help from parents and relatives, there are many who don't. It would be cruel and insensitive of me to place an unrealistic burden on them by telling them they shouldn't borrow in fact, it is quite ridiculous to even suggest it.

If you need a mortgage or furniture and you can afford the monthly instalments then borrow and don't feel *guilty* or *non-spiritual* about doing it! This is common sense and to suggest anything else and dress it up under the heading of **Faith** is wrong, in fact, it is **Foolishness**

I have encountered many Christians who are in bondage and in particular, ministers who are doing without and

PARALLEL TRUTH

depriving themselves and their families of basic home comforts, thinking that they are in obedience to God.

Do you really think God wants us to **deprive** our spouse and children – **does that sound like Jesus**? Many choose to go without thinking that in doing so, they are exercising Faith.

What about buying?

- **A nice home**
- **A bed**
- **Some furniture**
- **A car**

And have faith to believe God that your income will **remain steady** or perhaps **even increase** because of your needs. Does scripture not promise that **"God will supply all your needs"**?

And my God will meet all your needs according to His riches in Glory by Christ Jesus.
(Philippians 4v19)

It is foolishness to do without when you can have what you *need* if you have good credit and are working in a *steady job* – in fact, in those circumstances it does not make sense to deprive your family.

Chapter 7
Faith or Foolishness

I believe in Faith Principles.
I believe God wants us to exercise our faith.

However I also believe we are all *on a journey* and as such, have *different levels of faith* operating within the body of Christ. This is demonstrated even among the apostles – Peter was the only one who had the faith to walk on water.

It takes years of *perseverance, study* and *knowing God* to *develop* your faith. I must admit I am taken aback by some Christians' interpretation of faith, believing that with 'faith' they can have anything at all, with absolutely no application of **wisdom**.

Using Faith

If you really want to use faith wouldn't it be more *practical* to believe in the first instance for a *job*. There are many Christians out there who do not work, and yet are 'believing' to live a debt free life.

> *"If a man will not work, he will not eat. We hear that some among you are idle. They are not busy, they are busybodies. Such people we command*

BALANCING PROSPERITY PRINCIPLES

*and urge in the Lord Jesus Christ to **settle down and earn the bread that they eat**"*
   2nd Thessalonians 3:10-15

Paul did not say *if it fits your understanding of prosperity or your doctrine* . . . no he said, *"For even when we were with you, this we commanded."* Paul had first hand knowledge of these types of Christians.

I too have first hand knowledge as do many Pastors and members of the Body of Christ. Some Christians will simply not work, but yet persist in dressing it up as being somehow spiritual.

I cannot be more frank than this:- these people are badly misled in their thinking and many of them are just bone lazy. I have heard spiritual excuses dressed up under the guise of faith and it has to <u>STOP.</u>

Eat Their Own Bread

Now I don't want you to miss this!

The scripture states clearly that *"Every man ought to eat his own bread"*

In other words – **"you had better get yourself a JOB"** and earn your **own** money to buy your **own** provisions.

Let Your Faith Grow

As stated earlier we are all at different levels when it comes to our own faith. Of course the goal is to get to a place where you won't have to borrow and are living debt free. *However you don't just start there*. All of us have to grow and develop not only our faith but in life skills and wisdom.

FAITH OR FOOLISHNESS

What sounds easier to believe in; a monthly payment or a massive lump sum of capital?

For example, to buy a house at £100,000 and pay it cash, takes an incredible amount of money which most people do not have, and if you are believing God to supply it then it also takes alot of faith.

Is it not more *practical* and wise to believe God for the monthly payment of £600.00 to pay the mortgage?

The same example is true for other necessities in life, for example:

- **A car**
- **Furniture**
- **Television**
- **Washing machine**

Is a Mortgage Debt?

This is a subject that I have covered with many of my Christian clients who will not commit to a mortgage as they believe it is debt. However before I deal with this subject let us look at the **alternatives.**

Assuming you are married and perhaps have children you could fall into either of the categories below:

- **Living with parents**
- **Living with friends**
- **Renting**

Living With Parents

Sometimes this *is necessary* for young married couples at the beginning, but I do not believe it is a good choice and, I would *caution* against it on almost every occasion. The

BALANCING PROSPERITY PRINCIPLES

stress and strain this puts on everyone is not God's best and gives the *enemy a foothold* into bringing *division* into a family. I believe, in particular, from a practical point of view, women need to build their own nests and men need to be sensitive to their wives and provide a place for them to build the family home.

Two women sharing one kitchen can spell disaster!!!

Living with Friends

This may sound a good solution at the time and again, may be necessary at the beginning until a young couple can 'get on their feet' financially. You may think because your friends are of the same age group as you that you will be able to enjoy the company and even have fun together. However, the early years of marriage are the *most private* and *intimate* for a young couple and this should be respected. This is not God's best.

Renting

Again, this may be *necessary* at the beginning, but I do not believe it is best long term. I do understand that there are some of the older generation who have never ventured from their council house and it has been the family home for decades. However, now in the UK it is possible to *purchase your council house* and receive a *substantial discount as a condition of sale.*

This is known as '**Right to Buy**'. I believe this is a great opportunity to make a quick return on the purchase of your council house property. Many children who will eventually inherit this property willingly pay their parents mortgage allowing them to *live rent free* thereby blessing them in their old age but also *securing* a good long-term investment for themselves.

FAITH OR FOOLISHNESS

A Note Of Caution

I have to warn however that when well-intentioned family members wish to buy their parents' council house many mistakes can be made which can give the *enemy a foothold*. Therefore I would suggest that all the family meet together with an *Independent Financial Adviser and a Solicitor to ensure that all eventualities are covered.*

Private Rental

This too may be necessary, but I believe this is a poor option. Renting does not allow any investment for the tenant. I am sure we are all familiar with the saying:

'Throwing money down the drain'
with regard to renting.

This is where I would challenge those who claim to live by *Faith*. If you have to pay monthly rent why not believe God for the monthly payment on a mortgage?

Let me explain further in order to clarify that having a mortgage is a much *wiser* option!

When you rent, every time you pay the monthly payment, you are actually paying the landlord's mortgage (if he has one) or you are paying him an income. On the other hand, taking a mortgage out to buy your house is ***an investment***. Every time you make a payment, you are paying yourself something and over the years as the mortgage balance comes down ***your property value goes up***.

As I write this book, property values have **risen** on average by **20%** in the last year. That is an impressive return compared to the mortgage variable rate of **6.84%**. Can you see God's wisdom in this? Can you also see how

BALANCING PROSPERITY PRINCIPLES

the enemy would *confuse God's people by twisting scriptures to keep them in bondage.*

The World's System

Again this is an area of thinking that I believe I must tackle as so many are in confusion. I have heard it said that you must only *invest in God's system* and that investment in the world is not God's will. I do not know of any scripture that tells me categorically not to invest in the world's system.

What is Meant by the World's System?

This again is confusing to Christians, as we have all been taught *'not to do things by the world's standards'*. (Roman 12v2) is so often misconstrued.

> *Do not conform any longer to the patterns of this world, but be transformed by the renewing of the mind.*

However, this scripture *in context is relating to disobedience* and God's **mercy**. This has **nothing at all to do** with finances. Consider this: Banks are part of the world's system. Does this mean we have to withdraw our money and keep it under our bed.

- **Do you travel by car, boat or aeroplane? If so then you are taking part in the world's system**
- **Do you buy food from supermarkets?**
- **Clothes from shopping malls?**
- **Watch TV and movies ?**

The list is endless even using *gas and electricity* in our homes is part of the world's system.

FAITH OR FOOLISHNESS

If you are not going to use the world's system, then you are going to have to **STOP**:

- **Wearing clothes**
- **Wearing make-up**
- **Buying Food**
- **Turning on the lights**
- **Travelling**
- **Cooking**

Can you see how **ridiculous** this is?

I have lost count how many times I have heard Christians say *"I do not operate in the world's system and I'm proud of it"*, without any practical insight into what it is they are actually saying!!

Not My Portion

I have heard this statement used so many times by well-meaning Christians. However, again it has been *misused and misunderstood*.

I recently spoke to a pastor friend of mine who told me about a man who came to his Church. Whenever this man receives a bill through the post, he tears it up, declaring *"That's not my portion"* If anyone reading this book recognises themselves in that statement, then I'm sorry to let you know, *But it most certainly is your portion!!!* It is lacking in honour and integrity not to pay a bill for which **you** are responsible. If you have used electricity, gas or the telephone then you must pay up to the company concerned.

Life Insurance

I have also heard it said, concerning life insurance to protect mortgage payments and to provide protection for family members in the event of death.

BALANCING PROSPERITY PRINCIPLES

- That's not my portion
- I don't need life insurance
- God's angels are protecting me
- I'm walking by Faith

When a Christian client of mine refused life insurance, I tried to explain that this was necessary in the event of death to pay off the mortgage ensuring his wife and family had no hardship. He rejected this by saying he would live a long life, quoting **Psalm 91v16:** *With long life will I satisfy him and show him my salvation.* But does this guarantee that you will live a long life?

This scripture also states:

> *The righteous perish and no one ponders it in his heart. Devout men are taken away and no one understands that the righteous are taken away to be spared from evil. Those who walk uprightly enter into peace. They find rest as they lie in death.*
>
> ***Isaiah 57:1-2***

Notice this scripture is not talking of a yo-yo now and then, whenever I feel like it Christian with a whole lot of issues in tow. This is a righteous, devout follower of the Lord who *walks uprightly.*

The history of the church and the Martyrs are full of records of young men and women of God who died young whilst serving the Lord with all their hearts.

It also states in this scripture that *They are taken away* indicating that God takes them to spare them from future evil.

My own dear son died at the early age of eighteen months from leukaemia and my brother died aged forty-six years old.

FAITH OR FOOLISHNESS

- **We exercised our Faith**
- **We laid hands**
- **We anointed with oil**

But in the end they went home to be with Jesus.

Does this mean I don't believe in healing – **certainly NOT!**

I believe God heals!
I believe we can lay hands on the sick!

However, what I am simply trying to do once again is to **bring balance** and **common sense** which I believe will help set people free from wrong thinking and believing.

Chapter 8
Don't Give the Devil a Foothold

Eph 4v27

Think about the effect it would have on your spouse and children if you were to die whilst owing a mortgage and other lending.

I have witnessed first hand the devastation that occurs when this happens.

- The family house could be repossessed.

- Wife and family could be moved to rental property provided by the local council (perhaps a bad district).

- Children taken out of their own school and placed elsewhere.

- Wife has to pay off all liabilities.

- Wife has to work more hours to pay bills.

- Mother may be unable to take care of the children.

- Nervous breakdown may ensue.

BALANCING PROSPERITY PRINCIPLES

Now that is what I call giving the enemy a foothold.

Another example is car insurance. What would happen if the car you relied upon so heavily for work was written off in a car crash and you had no insurance.

I am sure all of us do not intend to have an accident, but even though we are blood bought anointed citizens of Heaven, we are still imperfect and live in an imperfect world. Just like you and me everyone else out there driving is imperfect.

<u>Notice:</u> Having car insurance does not stop the accident from happening but it does stop the devil from causing havoc in your personal and financial life.

I had personal experience whilst on holiday in Florida with my family. We had unwittingly broken the law by driving in an area where traffic was not allowed. The police pulled us over and lectured us on how we must obey Florida law. Therefore ignorance was no excuse.

The policeman checked our insurance documents and told us that we could have a *massive financial claim* against us if we collided with another car.

In America, if you do not have insurance you are leaving yourself open to law suit which could potentially ruin you financially.

This is not a negative confession, but merely a statement of fact. These things can happen in life and it is *foolish* not to have protection for your family.

Angelic Protection

I believe in angels, I believe God's messengers have intervened on numerous occasions on behalf of God's people.

DON'T GIVE THE DEVIL A FOOTHOLD

However, I also believe that God has given us free will and common sense to apply in our daily lives.

I always find it amusing when some Christians refuse life insurance stating that the angels are protecting them. But these same people *lock every door and window* in their house before they go to bed, together with their cars and garage.

My argument is *why lock up if your belief is that the angels are your protective force?*

The answer is simple:

We live in an *imperfect world* and there are some really *mean people* ready to take advantage of our foolishness.

Contents Insurance

The same principle applies as so many people have been killed as a direct result of a fire. Many have managed to escape but all their belongings and furniture have been consumed in the blaze. Thank God there are insurance policies to cover such an eventuality. Anyone could accidentally leave an oven on, or a candle burning. Anyone can mess up, however, by having this protection in place, *The Devil has no Foothold*.

Chapter 9

Why are Christians not Prospering?

I've had this discussion on so many occasions with close friends and fellow brothers and sisters who believe that God wants us to prosper. Many Christians are faithful tithers and givers and yet have never received the abundance that God promises in His Word.

Guilt and Condemnation

We know as believers that guilt and condemnation does not come from our Heavenly father. However, on this very subject so many have been told *"they must be doing something wrong"*. I do agree that there are situations where God in his mercy withholds his blessing from us. But what I am concerned and uneasy about is that God's people find themselves back under the law.

- **The law demands perfection**
- **The law demands total obedience**
- **The law punishes failure**

Thank God Jesus Christ came to *redeem us from the curse of the law (Gal 3v13)* bringing grace and truth and paying the price on Calvary's cross for all our sins and failures. By trying to obey every rule and formula set out by some well-intended pastors/preachers God's people have been wounded.

BALANCING PROSPERITY PRINCIPLES

I have heard countless stories regarding Christians who have been so confused by their pastor/teacher telling them that they are in disobedience when quite frankly they are not.

How many times each day do we all sin, how many times each day are we disobedient or rebellious even in our thinking (*Proverbs 24v16*)

A righteous man falls seven times daily.

We simply cannot condemn our brothers and sisters in Christ who are doing their best to follow the Lord Jesus Christ with all their heart, by telling them it's their fault.

Now I know there are instances when God will not prosper people and in particular, those who conceal sin and are unrepentant.

A man who conceals his sins does not prosper
(Prov 28v13).

A man of perverse heart does not prosper
(Prov 17v20)

The scripture also warns that:

. . . prosperity can ruin the fool.
(Prov 1v32)

Wisdom

Of what use is money in the hands of a fool, since he has no desire to get wisdom.
Proverbs 17v16

This is another key scripture I would like to share with reference to prosperity and it clearly states that we need to have wisdom when dealing with money.

WHY ARE CHRISTIANS NOT PROSPERING?

The Balance

I feel very strongly the need to teach people the **balance** of acquiring wisdom, as they **key** to prosperity. I have no desire to challenge anyone's doctrine and I am sure that there are numerous scriptures and stories that can be quoted with respect to Biblical Prosperity.

Financial Advice

However in all my studies, the books and tapes I have listened to over the years I have never heard of a reference to seeking qualified advice from a reliable Independent Financial Adviser. Why not?

Practical not Spiritual

Could it not be that most people are not prospering because they lack wisdom with respect to their finances?

In my experience I have to admit that the majority of Christians I have advised on their financial affairs were in great need of professional practical advice and had nothing to do with sin in their lives.

If the truth be told, how many Christians have no in depth knowledge about the following:

- **Mortgages**
- **Investments**
- **Raising Capital**
- **Credit Card Control**
- **Tax Avoidance**
- **Life Cover**

The answer is *the majority* and these are good law-abiding God loving Holy Ghost people who desire to prosper but just need the practical tools to be able to do so.

Chapter 10

Law versus Grace

In this chapter I want to encourage God's people in coming to the realisation that we have a wonderful Father who loves us and wants us to prosper by *Grace*, not by Law. Knowing faith and prosperity principles is meaningless if you do not know God and trust him.

Distorted View

When we don't know God and how he operates under grace then we are left with a distorted view and the enemy discredits the Lord by putting New Testament saints in 'bondage'. The only way you can truly know anything about God is through His Word. The fullest Revelation of God is not tradition or doctrine but the Word of God.

2nd Timothy 3v16

All scripture is God-breathed and is useful for:

- **Teaching**
- **Rebuking**
- **Correcting**
- **Training**

BALANCING PROSPERITY PRINCIPLES

*So that the man of God may be
thoroughly equipped for every good work.*

Opinions

So many Christians have an opinion when it comes to how God views money and prosperity. Just saying the word money in a crowd will arouse a variety of emotions: Some will have joy, others grief, others anger or guilt, jealousy, pain – even pride may avail.

However the only reliable source is the written Word of God. It seems when it comes to prosperity that God's people are confused as there seems to be an argument for and against many of the principles taught in our Churches.

Rightly Dividing

The scripture tells us that we must rightly divide the Word.

> *Do your best to present yourself to God as one approved, a workman who does not need to be ashamed and who rightly divides the Word of Truth.*
>
> 2nd *Tim 2v15*

In the Old Testament the picture of God is not incorrect, but merely incomplete. Therefore if your understanding of God is from the Old Testament alone then you do not have a fully accurate picture. The Old Testament is only part of the picture therefore we need to harmonise the New Testament with the Old to see the full picture.

Many religious and traditional ideas arise through a misunderstanding and misappropriation of the scriptures.

Matthew 22v29, Jesus replied: *"You are in error because you do not know the scriptures or the power of God"*

LAW VERSUS GRACE

"You have let go of the commands of God and are holding on to the traditions of men."
Mark 7v8

"Thus you nullify the word of God by your tradition that you have handed down".
Mark 7v13

" . . . are you so dull"
Mark 7 v18

"He said to them how foolish you are and how slow of heart to believe all the prophets have spoken. Did not the Christ have to suffer these things and then enter his glory and beginning with Moses and all the prophets, he explained to them what was said in all the scriptures concerning himself" v45:– "Then he opened their minds so they could understand the scriptures".
Luke 24:25 27

God's Character

Whoever does not love does not know God because God is Love.
1st John 4v8

Biblical Interpretation

The Number one Law of Biblical Interpretation is always to interpret the scripture with the character of God in mind and the Character of God is Love. Many believers today are seeing God through the Old Testament instead of through Jesus.

"The Son is the radiance of God's glory and the exact representation of his being. Sustaining all things by his powerful word". **Hebrews 1v3**

BALANCING PROSPERITY PRINCIPLES

The purpose of the law was to give knowledge of sin. God never wanted men to see him through fear of His wrath but by His Goodness.

> *"It's the goodness of God that should lead us to repentance"*
> **Romans 2v4**

Conviction draws people to God, but condemnation drives them away from God.

> *"Come to me all you who are weary and burdened and I will give you rest. Take my yoke upon you and learn from me for I am gentle and humble in heart and you will find rest for your souls for my yoke is easy and my burden is light".*
> **Matthew 11v28-30**

You see, the yoke of the Law is heavy.

The yoke of Grace is easy.

Attempting to try and keep the law brings burdens and heaviness – *we can't do it*!

> *"They tie up heavy loads and put them on many shoulders but they themselves are not willing to lift a finger to move them"*
> **Matthew 23v4**

> *"For whoever keeps the whole law and yet stumbles at just one point is guilty of breaking ALL of it."*
> **James 2 v10**

The grace and rest provided by Jesus is undeserved and unearned therefore if you feel burdened and heavy with respect to your finances you can be assured this is not what Jesus wants.

LAW VERSUS GRACE

The Church needs to be set free from the yoke of Old Testament thinking and the 'Performance Mentality' with respect to prosperity.

God didn't wait until we got our act together before he saved us.

> *For it is by Grace you have been saved through Faith and this not from yourself, it is the gift of God. It's not by works lest any man should boast.*
> ***Eph 2 v 8&9***

- **Abraham lied to Pharaoh**
- **Abraham took Hagar and had sex with her**
- **Abraham's wife Sarah, laughed at God**
- **Isaac lied about Rebekah, saying she was his sister**
- **Isaac manipulated**
- **Isaac was selfish**
- **Jacob was a liar**
- **Jacob was a cheat**
- **Jacob was a deceiver**
- **Jacob was a swindler**

But when God appeared to Moses (who was a murderer) He said: *"I am the God of Abraham, Isaac and Jacob"*.

He is the God of :−

- **The hopeless**
- **The helpless**
- **The alcoholic**
- **The addict**
- **The slanderer**
- **The murderer**
- **The abused**
- **The broken-hearted**
- **The backslider**

BALANCING PROSPERITY PRINCIPLES

- **The prisoner**
- **The prostitute**

God proved his love for mankind by dying for us whilst we were still sinners. (**Romans 5 v 8**) – *But God demonstrates His own love for us in this. While we were still sinners, Christ died for us.*

So don't be dragged back into Law:–

- **Stop trying to perform**
- **Stop feeling guilty**
- **Stop trying to impress**

He is the God who loves us and his mercies are new every morning and *His love is not based on performance.*

If this is the truth when it comes to our Salvation, then it has to be the truth when it comes to our Financial Prosperity.

The reason I felt compelled to write this chapter was to lay a foundation for God's people to know the *truth and bring balance* to the bondage so many find themselves in.

> *If the law/performance, is not a factor in receiving Salvation, neither is it a factor in receiving Financial Prosperity*

What I'm trying to say here is that no **formula or performance** is necessary for Financial Prosperity, because that would be taking us back to the Law. God, like any Father, will most certainly bless and provide for his children in their times of need. However, it is also necessary for us to be good stewards and seek wisdom in the daily outworking of our finances.

LAW VERSUS GRACE

Finally

"We can boldly go before the throne of grace to obtain mercy in our time of need".
Hebrew 4v16

Notice this scripture talks about our *'time of need'* not when we have fulfilled all the law or because we are perfect.

We approach the throne of grace not the throne of works not the throne of **perfect performance.**

THIS IS THE GLORIOUS GOSPEL

THIS IS THE GOOD NEWS

<u>'ALLELUIA'</u>

Chapter 11
Seeking Wise Counsel and Knowledge – Not a Formula

In today's society, we are bombarded with self-help messages. However, there are many Christians who would not acknowledge the practical outworking theories contained within these publications.

Whilst not endorsing all of this material, I have to admit that many of the principles being taught *are in parallel* with Scripture and are helping millions world-wide.

Seek God First

As Christians, we know that we must first seek God

> *Seek first the Kingdom of God and His righteousness, and all these things will be added unto you.*
> **Matt 6v33**

Prayer

> *Therefore, I tell that whatever you ask for in Prayer, believe that you have received it and it shall be yours.*
> **Mark 11 v 24**

BALANCING PROSPERITY PRINCIPLES

As you seek God first in Prayer, ask Him to lead you in seeking wise counsel in the area of prosperity.

> *He who walks with wise men will be wise, but the companion of fools will suffer harm.*
> **Proverbs 13v20**

All too often, Christians throw wisdom and caution to the wind, when it comes to taking advice. They have buried their heads in the sand whilst quoting faith scriptures.

Trust God and Act

Therefore as you move out in Faith, you need to take certain actions whilst expecting God to answer your Prayers.

> *To be mature is to be basic Christ, no more no less. That's what I am working so hard at day after day, year after year, doing my best with the energy God so generously gives me.*
> **Col:1v29** (The Message translation)

Respond to God's Leading

I'm sure you've heard this story many times but I feel it is prudent to illustrate how we must respond to who God sends into our lives:-

During a terrible flood, a Christian man had to climb onto his roof as the waters were rising. He prayed to God "Please rescue me and send me help".

Along came a man in a boat saying "get in, we will take you to safety."

The Christian replied *"no I'm waiting for God to rescue me."*

The waters were rising higher and higher.

Then came a man in a speedboat shouting "get in quickly" but the Christian said *"no, I've prayed that God will rescue me"*.

SEEKING WISE COUNSEL AND KNOWLEDGE – NOT A FORMULA

Then finally as the waters reached the rooftop, where he stood, a helicopter came along and a voice rang out "quick climb up on the ladder and we will take you to safety"

"No, replied the Christian, I've prayed and I expect God to answer."

Eventually, the waters covered the whole house and the man was drowned.

He went to Heaven and stood before the Lord and said "Lord, what happened, I prayed and prayed and I believed you were going to rescue me".

The Lord said " Well, what did you expect, I sent you two boats and a helicopter and *you did not respond to them."*

I believe that this story illustrates that we have the responsibility to respond to God's desire to send us professional help instead of spiritualising our financial breakthrough.

Get Rich Quick

I caution everyone not to fall for any '**Get Rich Quick**' scheme. I plead with the Body of Christ, to use wisdom and discernment when you hear of such teaching. In my business experience, I personally have never met anyone who has accumulated wealth overnight and who are also walking upright before God.

I do accept however, that Satan, has his agents in the world, who have acquired wealth due to organised crime, the selling of drugs, gambling, prostitution and many other sinful activities. The enemy knows how to appeal to our greed and the lust of our eyes. However, *the wages of sin is death:*

> *Such is the end of all who go after ill-gotten gain.*
> *It takes away the lives of those who get it.*
> **(Proverbs 1v19).**

BALANCING PROSPERITY PRINCIPLES

Be Diligent

God rewards our hard work and if we want to prosper God's way – Be Diligent.

Romans 12v11(Various translations)

- *Never lacking in zeal (NIV)*
- *Not slothful in business (KJ)*
- *Never slack in earnestness (WMS)*
- *Never be lazy in your work (TAY)*

Do the best you can at your job. Work harder and longer hours if necessary. Even change jobs if you can.

If you're married and your children are at school, or maybe grown up. Perhaps your wife could begin a new career or even her own business, doing something that she loves. Joy creates enthusiasm in your work.

Think Big

My own wife stepped out after much prayer and consideration from her Admin job, to become a **successful** property developer. Believe in yourself and trust in God.

Commit to Planning

God is **Creator**. We have all been made in the image and likeness of the Almighty who created the heavens and the earth.

> *Trust in God with all your heart and lean not on your own understanding. In all your ways acknowledge Him and He shall direct your plans.*
> **Proverbs 3v5 & 6**

SEEKING WISE COUNSEL AND KNOWLEDGE – NOT A FORMULA

Commit your work to the Lord and it shall succeed.
Proverbs 16v3 (TLB)

Pursue Knowledge

As I encourage you to rise up, I must also caution that you must have a *balanced approach* to your prosperity. I know many Christians today who have such passion and enthusiasm but have *no common sense*.

In their desire to follow God, they leave a trail of disaster and poor testimony to everyone they come in contact with.

I've preached for many years that it's time for the **Church to grow up**. I know that many believe it's time for Revival and for the Church to rise up and waken up. But what is the point if we just become **shallow zealots**. I'm sorry, but I've witnessed too much damage by Christians in the wake of this '**Charismania**'.

It is not good to have zeal without knowledge, nor to be hasty and miss the way.
Proverbs 19v3

He who works his land will have abundant food, but he who chases fantasies, lacks judgement.
Proverbs 12v11:-

The plans of the diligent lead to profit as surely as haste leads to poverty.
Proverbs 21v5

Meditate

I ask you to stop at this juncture and reflect on your financial position. In this busy world we very rarely sit down and just meditate.

BALANCING PROSPERITY PRINCIPLES

I want you to be perfectly honest with yourself and if married, your partner.

Have you been **inspired** and set free by what you have read so far.

Have you **identified** with some of the illustrations contained within this book.

Did you **feel condemned** in the **past** with respect to your finances.

If you answered yes to all three questions, then we have simply identified that you only **need some knowledge** in your financial affairs.

> *My people are destroyed for lack of knowledge.*
> **Hosea 4v6**

Destroyed means:-

- **To pull down**
- **To demolish**
- **To kill**

Knowledge means:-

- **To be well-informed**
- **To be aware of the facts**
- **To have understanding**
- **To be sure of**
- **To have securely in the memory**

To paraphrase, knowledge is as follows **All the facts and range of information pertaining to a person or subject**.

Again it is important to understand the context of this scripture. When reading at first it would seem that God's people were to blame for their lack of knowledge. However, if you look at the background information and previous verses you will find that the priests were living

SEEKING WISE COUNSEL AND KNOWLEDGE – NOT A FORMULA

in **neglect** of their duty. **The people bring charges against them for not teaching them the knowledge of God.**

I believe this is what has happened in our Churches and in particular with some prosperity teachers. God's people are lacking in **practical knowledge** and their teachers have neglected their responsibility to address this balance.

I am a great believer in **Life Application Teaching** – God's people need His wisdom for today's world not yesterdays world – not tradition and certainly we don't need to be **spiritualising every single subject.**

> *The teacher imparted knowledge to the people.*
> *ECC 12v9*

> *Where there is no vision the people perish.*
> ***Proverbs 29v18***

You see ignorance can be very destructive and lack of knowledge can ruin a people.

I am encouraged today that a **new breed of teachers** have been raised up by God to bring dynamic life application teaching to the Body of Christ and the evidence of this is **explosive church growth.**

Today God has called for a 21st century church experience which is God-centred, prophetic in nature, relevant, people-empowering and purpose filled.

I have a general rule of thumb, when discerning whether a person has knowledge of a subject. I usually observe **their conduct** to see if there is any evidence to suggest that they really do know what they're talking about. If a person is erratic and unorganised in the area of finances, then it would generally suggest that they lack **knowledge within that particular area.**

BALANCING PROSPERITY PRINCIPLES

Knowing God

The same principle works when discerning someone's knowledge of God. The knowledge they have will be applied to their own lives and will be evident for all to see.

Where God is NOT Known, there will be:

- **Habitual sin**
- **Backbiting and Gossiping**
- **Selfishness**
- **Pride**
- **Jealousy**
- **Unforgiveness**
- **Bitterness**

You can still be Born Again and yet still not **truly know** God

Where God IS Known, there will be:

- **Servanthood**
- **A Forgiving Heart**
- **A Merciful Spirit**
- **Joy**
- **Peace**
- **A Disciplined Lifestyle**
- **Tenderness**

Therefore my people will go into exile for lack of understanding.
Isaiah 5v13

Again the scripture tells us about the importance of having knowledge and understanding.

SEEKING WISE COUNSEL AND KNOWLEDGE – NOT A FORMULA

Exile

I feel it's worth highlighting that the word 'exile' in the context of this scripture means:-

'A prolonged enforced way of living'

Do you feel or have you felt this same exile in the area of your finances?

> *The ox knows his master, the donkey his owners manger but Israel does not know. My people do not understand.*
>
> *Isaiah 1v3*

Please don't miss this! God uses the example of an ox and a donkey to describe his people. It's well known and understood that these animals are generally **very** *stupid and stubborn*.

The Bible is a handbook towards the abundant life God wants us to enjoy. **Money management** is crucial to a believer's financial stewardship.

In my experience as a financial adviser, the majority of Christians have been lacking in knowledge and have needed **practical guidance** in their finances. This I can accept when I have been approached for advice. However some Christians with an exaggerated zeal and wanting an **'all things spiritual' approach,** have been as stubborn as the **ox and the mule.**

Wealth Comes Through Knowledge and Diligence

Too often, people want to get 'something for nothing'. They tend to look for a **shortcut to wealth**. The Bible tells us that a key advancement in life is to develop our skills and then do the best we can at what we do well.

BALANCING PROSPERITY PRINCIPLES

Do you see a man who excels in his work? He will stand before Kings, he will not stand before unknown men.
Proverbs 22v9

Weigh up all counsel given !

A simple man believes anything but a prudent man gives thought to his steps.
Proverbs 14v15

The purpose of advice is to offer suggestions, alternatives and options. A good financial adviser will listen closely and prepare for his recommendations. It is not his job to make decisions on your behalf, so beware of **'the pushy type'**.

It is so important that you make sound and wise financial decisions. Therefore, you should always **pray** before any final decision is made.

As I stated earlier, *'The Peace of God'* is our umpire. In other words, this peace or lack of it, is an indisputable indicator of God's direction.

Referrals

I've found that the best method for locating a good financial adviser is by 'word of mouth'. Ask your friends, pastors, and Christian business people, who it is they like to deal with.

Independent

It's worth noting at the moment, that there are different types of adviser:-
- **Tied**
- **Multi-Tied**
- **Independent**

SEEKING WISE COUNSEL AND KNOWLEDGE – NOT A FORMULA

Tied Advisers:– These are financial advisers who are working for a bank, building society or a major insurance company. They are limited, as they can only recommend and sell products from the company they represent.

Multi-Tied Advisers:– These advisers can offer products from more than one provider, but they are limited and are not totally independent.

Independent Financial Advisers:– I would recommend an independent adviser on all occasions. They can advise on and recommend products from the 'whole market'

The best way I can illustrate the difference is using the analogy of **'the corner shop'** and **'the supermarket'**

More Choice

By going to a bank or an insurance company for a mortgage, insurance policy or investment, you are limiting your choice. This is similar to shopping at the local corner shop. There is no variety and the products are normally more expensive. However, by using an Independent Adviser, you have a variety of products, lenders and investment companies to choose from. The independent adviser has no limit and can search the whole market for the best and the cheapest product to suit your circumstances.

Chapter 12
A Dose of Reality

My own personal Testimony includes the roller-coaster of life together with all of the emotions involved. When I first studied Prosperity Teaching and the Abundant Life, I was so excited. However, my life experience has been that there is **another side to the abundant life.** I've preached about Victorious Living and I believe with all my heart that Jesus offers a life of overwhelming and overcoming abundance.

> *I have come that you may have life and have it more abundantly.*
> **John 10v10**

As followers of Jesus Christ, if we take this truth on its own, we will be headed for *disappointment, frustration and misery.*

Most Christians today when speaking about the saints of the past, tend to dwell on their victorious ministry, but the Scriptures tell us together with tradition that all people have a **secret history with God.** We tend to focus on the mountain top experiences, but never find out about **the valleys** these saints have been in and how they climbed to the top. In today's world, people are looking for **instant gratification** and I'm sad to say that this has crept into the Body of Christ.

BALANCING PROSPERITY PRINCIPLES

What's Wrong with Me?

Many saints are flocking to conferences, looking for the *instant touch*, the *instant change*, the *instant healing*. This type of thinking, rather than setting us free, can place us in bondage because the majority will never attain this Utopia and are left with a feeling of guilt. A famous doctor once said:

> *"What today's generation are looking for, is a medicine that will make it unnecessary for them to change their lifestyle, so that they can go on living in accordance with their whims and passions"*

This same philosophy is prevalent, particularly within the Charismatic/Pentecostal Church:-

- **Maybe this set of tapes will help me**
- **Maybe this video**
- **Maybe this seminar**
- **Maybe this book**

We want all of our problems to be fixed and *a disciplined approach to life can be extremely inconvenient.*

I believe that the Church really needs to **awaken** from this type of thinking. All of my Christian life I have been through crisis after crisis and every time I find myself saying:-

- **This will never happen again**
- **I've been through enough**
- **I've paid my dues**
- **I've suffered too much**
- **I've been too broken**

And as I reflect on my life to date, I only now realise that I was trying to convince myself after each situation

A DOSE OF REALITY

that I had got the *'all clear'*. However, instead, another *storm arose*.

Life's Experience

My Spiritual experience has been one of having a knowledge of God and of the Truth, particularly in the area of prosperity. I thought that I had every area covered – Then, *Blast!!!*

- **A total shake up**
- **Conflict**
- **My Theology questioned**
- **My Security in God challenged**

To sum up:– I have found that throughout my life there can be equally true, but opposing facts. My son died with leukaemia and yet in the midst of this tragic situation, I had no explanations, only my faith and trust in God. *A sense of His awesome presence* was all around me. My son's short life brought Salvation and conversion to not just my family and myself but to hundreds through my ministry and testimony.

At the time of his illness, it was the practical love and support of family and friends which carried me through this difficult time.

At the age of 30 my career ended suddenly and I found myself looking for employment. The fear was real. I can remember the nauseating stomach-churning feeling I had back then. However again through the love of God's people and practical financial support I was helped, until God miraculously opened a new door of opportunity, through a high street bank. In the first year with my new employers I paid more in tax than what I was paid as a salary from my previous employment. It was an exciting time. I was so hungry for God. I had experienced the

BALANCING PROSPERITY PRINCIPLES

spiritual highs and lows. I had a great sense of hope and passion for the Body of Christ.

However, I quickly realised that my spiritual beliefs and the reality of God's love in my life was not evident in all Christians.

I witnessed Christians with such spiritual knowledge tear others apart because of opposing doctrine.

I had been brought up in a traditional denomination which had been the subject of a special visitation by the Holy Spirit known as The Charismatic Renewal. The Baptism of Love was wonderful, however I had no idea that other Christians could be so cruel. I was being told to get out of my then denomination so vehemently, and at the same time being told by my family and friends that I should stay in?

Despite the arguments on both sides and all the spiritual reasoning, where was the practical love?

I moved to a new church and was so excited about the worship, the teaching, preaching and the fellowship. However I realised that we had become so good at meetings but had not outreached to the community. *So where then, was the practical love?*

I started to organise Evangelistic crusades, training and discipling people to reach the lost by just loving them in practical ways.

I quickly realised that many Christians were so super-spiritual, but had no idea how to reach out to a lost and dying world.

- **I had a deeper prayer life**
- **I loved to worship**
- **I loved to study the Word of God**

A DOSE OF REALITY

However I knew that the practical aspects of my faith were vital, not only in my own personal growth but in my communication with others.

I pioneered a new fellowship starting with just twenty people and growing to two-hundred-and-fifty. Our vision was to bring a message of *love and unity*, reaching the lost and broken-hearted.

We opened a coffee shop and we were reaching out to the lost, many drug addicts came and were powerfully saved. The one-parent families were coming, the hopeless and helpless were coming, not just because of spiritual truth but because a practical outworking of God's Love was there for all to obtain.

I believe with all my heart that it is the practical as well as the spiritual which brings success to the body of Christ. I can guarantee that – the new 21st century churches God is raising up – you will find various practical ministries reaching the community or city they are in.

The preaching and teaching will be scripturally sound but so practical and applicable in the lives of the congregation.

I've included this personal testimony to validate my strong belief in *bringing the balance between the spiritual and the practical.*

Our dreams and our adventures are wonderful, but so are our *battles*, as well as our *blessings!*

We can't read the book of dreams without also reading the book of reality.

CONCLUSION

This book has been written in the first instance, to reach people who believe in Biblical Prosperity. Whether that be tithing, sowing, or giving generously. I felt compelled to address many issues, which I believe has held the Body of Christ captive in the whole area of Prosperity.

Too many have over-spiritualised this subject from the pulpit to the pews.

True financial success is financial freedom where we are at rest and peace.

We have the freedom not to be bound by guilt or condemnation.

We have the freedom to take care of our own families and not to worry about financial matters.

It is my heartfelt prayer that you have been set free from the yoke of bondage. I trust that you will come to the conclusion that your own prosperous future is not dependent, on a set of rules or a formula, but in gaining **wisdom.**

Scriptures on Biblical Principles and Practical Prosperity

Index

The Bible has a lot to say about practical issues of money and finances. Here are a few Scriptures on financial topics to get you started. There are 2350 Scriptures related to the handling of finances!

Accounting

Matthew	18:23-35
Matthew	25:14-30

Budgeting and Planning

Proverbs	22:3
Proverbs	24:3-4
Proverbs	27:12
Proverbs	27:23
Luke	12:16-21
Luke	14:28-30
Luke	16:1-8
1 Corinthians	16:1-2

BALANCING PROSPERITY PRINCIPLES

*Business Life
Attitudes and Actions*

Leviticus	19:12
Psalm	112:5
Proverbs	10:4
Proverbs	13:4
Proverbs	13:11
Ecclesiastes	5:12
Malachi	3:5
Luke	6:35a
Romans	12:11
Ephesians	4:28

Honesty Versus Unjust Gain

Deuteronomy	25:15
Proverbs	11:1
Proverbs	16:8
Proverbs	22:16
Proverbs	28:8
Jeremiah	22:13
Luke	16:10

Contentment

Luke	3:14
2 Corinthians	6:10
Philippians	4:11 & 12
1 Timothy	6:6-10
Hebrews	13:5

Cosigning Notes

Proverbs	6:1-5
Proverbs	11:15
Proverbs	17:18
Proverbs	22:26

INDEX

Debt

Deuteronomy	15:6
Psalm	37:21
Proverbs	3:27-28
Proverbs	22:7
Romans	13:8

Discipline

2 Corinthians	8:11
Hebrews	12:11

Facts

Proverbs	14:8-15
Proverbs	18:13
Proverbs	19:2
Proverbs	27:23-24
Luke	14:31-32

Inheritance

Proverbs	13:22
Proverbs	17:2
Proverbs	20:21
Ecclesiastes	2:18-19
Ezekiel	46:16-18
Luke	15:11-31

Investments

Proverbs	24:27
Matthew	25:14-30
2 Peter	3:10

BALANCING PROSPERITY PRINCIPLES

Money

Luke   16:1-13

Needs

Matthew   6:25-33

Planning

Genesis   37-41 – Joseph's example
Proverbs   21:5

Prosperity

Genesis   39:3
2 Chronicles   31:21
Psalm   1:1-3
Psalm   35:27
Proverbs   10:22
Proverbs   28:13
Jeremiah   17:8-10
2 Corinthians 8:1-15
Philippians   4:19

Provision

Genesis   41 – X
           (*Provision through a plan*)
Exodus   15 – Moses
1 Kings   17 – Elijah
2 Kings   4 – Elisha
John   21:2-6 – Peter
Matthew   4:11 – Jesus
Luke   12:7 – His People

INDEX

Prudence (Wisdom)

Psalm	112:5
Proverbs	8:12
Proverbs	12:16, 23
Proverbs 1	3:16
Proverbs	14:8,15,18
Proverbs	15:5
Proverbs	16:21
Proverbs	18:15
Proverbs	22:3
Proverbs	27:12
Hosea	14:9
Amos	5:12-13

Saving

Proverbs	21:20
Proverbs	30:24-25

Slothfulness

Proverbs	18:9
Proverbs	24:30-34
Ecclesiastes	10:18
2 Thessalonians	3:11-12
Hebrews	6:12

Speculation (Get-Rich-Quick Schemes)

Proverbs	12:11
Proverbs	13:11
Proverbs	14:15
Proverbs	19:2
Proverbs	21:5
Proverbs	23:4
Proverbs	28:19-20
Ecclesiastes	5:15-17

BALANCING PROSPERITY PRINCIPLES

Tithing and Giving

Deuteronomy	14:23
Proverbs	3:9 and 10
Malachi	3:10
Matthew	23:23
1 Corinthians	16:1-2
2 Corinthians	8:13-14
2 Corinthians	9:6-8
Hebrews	7:1-2

Waste

Luke	15:13
John	6:12

Wealth

Deuteronomy	8
Psalm	50:10-12
Proverbs	30:8-9
Ecclesiastes	2:26
Luke	12:16-21

Practical Prosperity:
General Course Content

The seminar will provide delegates with the essential information and cost cutting strategies to improve their financial status.

Who should attend?
Everyone who wants to have the practical knowledge to implement the basic principles of Practical Prosperity.

Course Content:–
- Introduction
- Background Information to Practical Prosperity
- Mortgages
- Switching Mortgages
- Investing in Property
- Savings and Investments
- Protecting Your Assets

> "This one day course will change your life forever"

> There will be an opportunity at the end of this session for a question and answer time.

Delegates will learn how to:–
- Understand all types of Mortgage Products
- Plan how to improve on their current Mortgage Payments
- Decide on what strategy to implement
- Grasp the essentials on Savings and Investments
- Be structured in their approach to their finances
- Build a Property Portfolio
- Reduce their liabilities
- Protect their families from financial hardship

Practical Prosperity:
Private Coaching

In a busy world, many people do not find the time to seek advice on financial matters. For this reason, I have decided to incorporate coaching on a one to one basis for those who need a more personal approach.

Session's will last one hour, by telephone, at the low cost of £40. You will be AMAZED at how much information you will receive on HOW TO PROSPER. On a professional level this type of coaching would normally cost between £100-£250. A pay up plan is also available for those on a tight budget.

Practical Prosperity coaching begins with a background information session conducted by email, during which we will cover the following:

- Current financial status
- Financial goals
- Worries and fears
- Why are you not prospering?
- What would you like to achieve from your sessions?

After I have received this information we can then schedule a time and date for our one to one personal telephone session.

All sessions will start and end with prayer as we believe that the Holy Spirit will divinely inspire our time together.

My job is to help you, inspire and encourage you to take the correct steps towards your dreams and desires.

I will not be recommending any financial institution or financial product. This advice should be sought by a regulated financial adviser.

Hosting Your Church Seminar?
Contact Details and Seminar Types

- General Seminar

- Debt Strategy

- Long Term Care

- Inheritance Tax

- Engaged and Married Couples

- Bible Students

- Misunderstood Texts Relating to Debt and Proserity

- Breaking the Cycle of Debt by Applying Wisdom

- Avoiding 'Get Rich Quick' Theories

- Prayer, Planning and patience

- Learning the difference Between Being Prompted and Pressured

Tel: 01475 686 202
Fax: 01475 686 530
email: t-quinn@btconnect.com
Web: www.practicalprosperity.co.uk
Address: 8 Main Street, Largs, Ayrshire, KA30 8AB

All you need to know about Mortgages

This book provides generic information to allow the reader to make informed choices. It is important today to not only have the knowledge but to implement what you have learnt. My prayer is that as you learn about all aspects of mortgages – your financial prosperity will be enhanced as you take the recommended action.

Price £2.99

Visit the website to order this book
www.practicalprosperity.co.uk